Shocking Science

5,000 years of mishaps and misunderstandings

ILLUSTRATED BY
John Kelly

WRITTEN BY
Steve Parker

HAMLYN

Editor: Andrew Farrow
Designer: Cathy Tincknell
Production Controller: Christine Campbell

First published in Great Britain 1996
by Hamlyn Children's Books,
an imprint of Reed Books,
Michelin House, 81 Fulham Road, London SW3 6RB,
and Auckland, Melbourne, Singapore and Toronto.

Illustrations copyright © 1996 John R. Kelly
Text copyright © 1996 Reed International Books Limited

ISBN 0 600 58557 3 (Hardback)
0 600 58558 1 (Paperback)

A CIP catalogue record for this book is available at the British Library.

Printed and bound in China
Produced by Mandarin Offset Ltd.

Contents

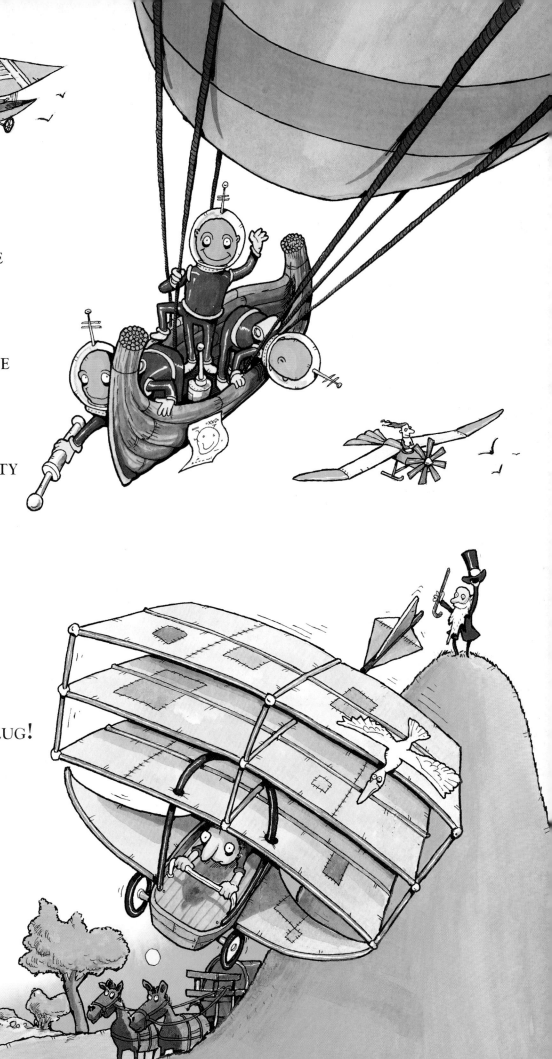

Shocking Science

Scientists are marvellous. They have produced all manner of wonders, from space probes to miraculous medical drugs. Scientists are sensible, sober, reliable people. They work methodically and rationally, in search of ultimate truth and understanding. They would never do anything stupid or surprising to startle or shock us. Oh yeah? Read on...

UNBELIEVABLE

Scientists mess up occasionally, like everyone else. They have misunderstood the world about them, ignored evidence, lusted after fame and fortune, and just plain got it wrong. This book takes the lid off science through the ages, to reveal blunders, hoaxes, unlucky accidents and bizarre beliefs. Some were harmless, and now raise a snigger. Others were truly shocking and resulted in wasted time and effort, and even tragic loss of life.

UNDERSTANDABLE?

The first people who tried to understand the Universe were called 'natural philosophers'. They studied stars, rocks, plants, animals and other aspects of the natural world. Modern branches of science, like astronomy, physics and genetics, developed because these scholars tried to find out about the world they lived in.

Now we can look back and smile at the odd ideas and funny beliefs of the past. In years to come, will people smile at us, with our odd ideas and funny beliefs?

It's just a programme about the Stone Age

UNFORGETTABLE?

Even a towering scientific genius like Isaac Newton was at the mercy of fate's little twists. He wrote careful notes and mathematical equations – but it is said that his dog knocked over a candle and burned the papers. Isaac had to remember bits and pieces for his monumental book on mathematics, the *Principia Mathematica*, which revolutionized much of science. If his dog had been less clumsy, might science have progressed even further?

UNREPEATABLE

In the early 1990s, two scientists reported that they had succeeded with 'cold fusion'. They could produce energy from a test-tube of special water, without the draw-backs of the usual 'hot fission' used in nuclear power stations. Limitless power from a cup of cold water? An end to all our energy and pollution problems? Despite hours of experiments and millions of dollars, nobody else has managed to repeat the results.

UNFORGIVABLE

In the 1970s, scientists were startled to hear that a Russian researcher had successfully transplanted furry skin from black mice to white mice. What an amazing breakthrough in medical science! If we could prevent a living body rejecting the tissue of a transplanted part, transplants would be more successful. Then it was discovered the researcher had drawn black patches on the white mice with a felt-tip pen.

I think there's something you should know

In the Beginning

In the beginning, what was there? A black hole? A supreme being? A giant dragon? Through the ages, legends and religions have told us about the beginning of the Universe and our own Earth and Sun. Today's scientists think they are much nearer to the answers. But hundreds of years ago scientists thought *they* were near the truth – and it was very different...

THE COSMIC EGG

In ancient Greece, some people believed that the gods created the heavens and Earth. Others said the world had always existed. Nearly 2,000 years ago, a Chinese myth told how the world was sculpted by a newly-hatched giant. 'First there was the great cosmic egg. Inside...was P'an Ku, the Divine Embryo. And P'an Ku burst from the egg...With a hammer and chisel in his hands, he fashioned the world.' This idea of the Earth, hatching or growing from an egg, was common to many ancient beliefs.

30 days hath September...

A NINE O'CLOCK START

The Bible of Christian religions tells how the heavens and Earth, and all living things, were made by God in six days. In 1650, Irish bishop James Ussher traced through the people in the Bible, and calculated their dates of birth. His work was improved by John Lightfoot into an official timetable of Creation. It stated the Earth was made at nine o'clock in the morning on 26 October, in 4004 BC. This was added to the Bible, becoming an accepted part of the great book for many years.

One for you, one for me...

SUDDENLY GROWING OLD

Until the early 1800s, most scientists believed the Catastrophe Theory. This said that the Earth, and its oceans and mountains, had been formed by great floods and other catastrophes described in the Bible. Scottish geologist James Hutton saw how slowly rocks formed and wore away. He guessed this had been happening since the Earth began, and so the Earth must be *incredibly* old. Hutton's *Theory of the Earth* was published in 1795. But its style was so boring, and its suggestions seemed so crazy, that most people ignored it.

OLDER AND OLDER

A few scientists did develop Hutton's ideas, and by the 1850s they believed the Earth was more than 6,000 years old. So what age was it?

⊕ In the mid-18th century, French naturalist Comte de Buffon said the Earth had cooled from red-hot rocks. By testing the cooling rate of iron balls, he estimated it was 75,000 years old.

🎓 Next, Scottish physicist William Thomson calculated its age at nearer 100 million years.

⚛ By 1907 the age of the Earth had leaped to 410 million years. In the 1930s it was at least 1,000 million years old.

1 0 0 0 0 0 0 0 0

THE BIGGEST BANG

Today, science's view is that the Universe came into being about 15,000 million years ago. It began when a tiny speck containing all matter blew up in a 'Big Bang'. The Sun, Earth and other planets formed around 4,600 million years ago, probably from clouds of gas and dust whirling in space.

At least, that's the *current* view...

Heavenly Motion

For thousands of years, people have lain on their backs and gazed at the night sky. Were the Moon and stars small and near, or large and far away? Why did they move in the same regular pattern? And why did...yawn...snore... (These great mysteries were a wonderful cure for sleeplessness.)

PERFECT CIRCLES

From the beginning, most people assumed the Earth was at the centre of everything. The Sun, Moon and stars went around us. And why not? It certainly looked that way. Ancient Greeks such as Aristotle believed that stars and other heavenly bodies moved in perfect circles. And there could be no movement unless one thing provided the moving force – God. Then...

...CRYSTAL BALLS

In ancient Egypt, the scientist Ptolemy added to Greek ideas on astronomy. He said the Sun, Moon and stars were fixed to crystal spheres – vast, thin-walled balls of a clear substance. But to fit with real observations of the stars, Ptolemy needed 80 crystal spheres, all turning different ways! Still, lots of people liked Ptolemy's perfect spheres, because God would surely have made a heavenly system as marvellous as this. Ptolemy's Earth-centred system dominated astronomy for 1,400 years. Until...

8

...THE SUN AT THE CENTRE

But Polish astronomer Nicolaus Copernicus said the Earth (and other planets) went round the Sun! His book, published in 1543, even said that the Earth spun around like a top!! This Sun-centred system was much simpler and more sensible than Ptolemy's complicated spheres. The Roman Catholic Church was horrified. It believed that God had made the Earth as the centre of the Universe. It forbade people to mention Copernicus' ideas. Meanwhile...

...OVAL ORBITS

German scientist Johannes Kepler had studied the planet Mars. He realized that the Earth and other planets *did* orbit the Sun – but not in perfect heavenly circles. In 1609 he proposed that the planets moved around the Sun in ellipses, or ovals. And then...

...A MOVING EARTH

So far, nobody had used a telescope, because it wasn't invented until 1608! At once, brilliant Italian all-rounder Galileo Galilei star-gazed through one. He saw mountains on the Moon, stars too faint for the naked eye – and four moons going round the giant planet Jupiter.

This was the first direct proof that the Earth was not the centre of everything. So Galileo spoke out in support of Copernicus. In 1633 the Church summoned him to Rome. It told him to admit the Earth *was* the centre and *did not move*. He was forced to agree, although legend says that, as he left, he muttered about the Earth: 'But it *does* move.' (Actually he would have said *Eppur si muove*, since he was Italian.)

Final Apology

Galileo was sentenced to house arrest for life. The Church ordered his books burned, and banned his teachings. Exactly 360 years later the Pope and Catholic Church finally said sorry, and admitted that Galileo had been right all along.

9

Mapping the Earth

Modern science tells us that space is not straight. It curves due to the gravity of massive objects such as stars. Is this idea hard to grasp? Then think how early scientists felt. A few people said the Earth was round. What a crazy idea! Everyone knew the Earth was flat...

CENTRED ON THE MED

In the time of the Greek poet Homer, almost 3,000 years ago, maps showed the Mediterranean Sea in the centre of a flat world. There were empty lands around it, then ocean. Beyond that...no-one knew!

STICKS AND SHADOWS

Then, about 2,200 years ago in ancient Egypt, the poet and scientist Eratosthenes became curious about a small problem. At noon on 21 June each year, in the city of Syene, the Sun was directly overhead. Its rays shone straight down a deep well. Yet in Alexandria, to the north, the rays did not shine straight down. They cast shadows on a tall obelisk.

Eratosthenes reasoned the Earth was not flat, but perhaps round like a ball. So he hired a man to pace out the distance between the two cities: 800 km. From this, Eratosthenes calculated it was 40,000 km around the Earth. He was not far out. But gradually many people forgot his work and went back to the idea of a flat Earth.

20,752, 20,753, 20,7... err... oh, #~**>#!

A ROUND WORLD

About 300 years later, the Egyptian scientist Ptolemy developed some Greek ideas. In his book *Geography* he returned to the idea of a ball-shaped Earth. Europe, North Africa and the Middle East now had a fairly realistic shape. But Ptolemy's map did not show any land below the equator, which he drew too far north.

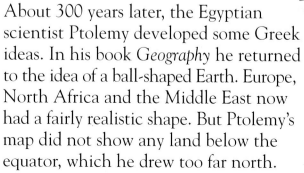

TAKING SHAPE

By the medieval period, about AD 1000, Arab geographers had used information from sailors and merchants to build up a fairly good map of the northern world. They added details of China and other Eastern lands where they traded silks and spices. They did not really know about the Americas. However, they suspected there was a great southern continent, a mixture of Australia and Antarctica!

RISKY ROUND THE EDGES

Meanwhile, in Europe, maps had taken several steps backwards. They were usually mixed up with religion and superstition. Most depicted a flat Earth with the holy city of Jerusalem at the centre. Many maps showed God looking down on the world. In the less-well known areas to the east and south, map-makers drew demons and fierce warriors waiting to invade Christian lands on behalf of the Devil.

How about this?

NEARLY ROUND

By the time Christopher Columbus arrived in the Americas, in 1492, most scholars had accepted that the Earth was round. We now know the Earth is not in fact a perfect sphere. It's more like a flattened pear. The distance round the Equator (40,075 km) is 67 km more than the distance around the two Poles. And the North Pole is 45 metres more pointed than the South Pole.

Dangerous Lands

In ancient times, people believed they were at the centre of the world. They thought that beyond their own region were strange and dangerous lands and oceans...

SEAS AND PLUGHOLES

Many early peoples said that their lands were surrounded by a great river or ocean. Sail across it, and the sea poured in a vast whirlpool, down a gigantic plughole into the blackness. The idea of a whirlpool made sense. Otherwise, surely rain would eventually fill up the oceans, and they would flood over the land?

HERE BE DRAGONS!

Some people believed that distant seas and lands were populated by massive dragons and serpents that breathed fire and ate unlucky travellers for breakfast. Sometimes they saw the dragon's smoke and fire far in the distance, and heard it roaring. Perhaps the rumbling and smoke were from a volcano?

WHEELS AND MOTIONS

Medieval storytellers described how a curious man travelled to the end of the flat Earth and poked his head through the curtain that was the sky. On the other side he saw the wheels and gears and levers which moved the Sun, Moon and stars. But the gods were angry at this intrusion. They mended the curtain, trapping the man by the neck, and he died.

How very interesting

THE SUN'S JOURNEY

In ancient Egypt, there were many beliefs about the Sun. Some said that it was pushed across the sky by an enormous scarab beetle. At dusk, it was swallowed by the sky goddess Nut, passing through her body until it was born again the next morning.

Oh well, here we go again...

In a box

Cosmas, a geographer from Egypt, drew the world in a huge box, with the heavens in its bulging lid. Day and night were created by a huge mountain that obscured the Sun for part of its journey.

SONGS FROM THE SEA

In Greek legends, sailors were lured to their deaths by three Sirens who sang beautiful songs from rocky islands. Each had the upper body of a woman, and the lower half of a bird. In European folklore, some mermaids sang lovely but deadly songs. Others were kind, saving sailors from shipwreck. Mermaids had the upper body of a woman, and the lower body and tail of a fish.

Monstrous People

More blood and stones anyone?

I n the 16th century, a person on the island of Ceylon (Sri Lanka) saw a strange sight: 'In harbour are some very white and beautiful people, who wear boots and hats of iron and never stay in any place. They eat a sort of white stone and drink blood.' Were they demons from the lower hells? Servants of the gods? Or Europeans, wearing metal helmets, eating bread and drinking wine..?

PLINY'S PEOPLE

One of the most important scholars of Roman times was Pliny the Elder. At dinner parties, Pliny 'entertained' his guests with some of the 20,000 facts in his 37-volume encyclopedia *Historia Naturalis*. These 'facts' included tales of peoples that lived in distant lands – such as the sciopods, who used their one huge foot to shade themselves from the Sun. There were also people with dogs' heads (called cynocephali); faces on their chests (the blemmyae, who lived in Africa); and even ones with huge ears for sleeping in and flying (the panotii, of the All Ears Islands).

What is it?

SCHOLARLY DEBATE

These peoples kept scholars arguing for centuries. In the 12th century, the Church even debated if it was possible to convert the dog-headed people of India to Christianity! The books of epic Venetian traveller Marco Polo, from the late 13th century, also included amazing tales of humanoid monsters. But, as always, there was no proper proof.

So do they live around here?

A STRANGE NEW WORLD?

Then, in 1492, Christopher Columbus made his first great voyage of exploration. Instead of finding the riches of the East, he found a 'New World' of lands not on the maps, the Americas. Surely this was where these monstrous people lived? But Columbus found no such monsters. He wrote with great honesty: 'The people are very well-formed, with handsome bodies and very fine faces.'

But people in Europe wanted to believe in human monsters. Despite Columbus' honesty, European scholars continued to tell stories about hideous creatures living on other continents. In the mid-16th century, books still showed sciopods living in India!

Hello?

HUGE, HAIRY BRUTES

Even today, according to some Himalayan peoples, the Yeti or Abominable Snowman roams their snowy mountains. In 1921, English explorers claimed to have found this huge, hairy creature's footprints. A similar beast is the Sasquatch or Bigfoot from the forests of north-west North America, or the swamps of south-eastern USA. Again, the evidence includes footprints, some shadowy photographs, and bits of fur.

15

More Mapping Madness

In about AD 1000, Egyptian scientist Alhazen boasted to his ruler, the Caliph, that he could build a dam across the upper River Nile. This would prevent flooding and store water for crops. The Caliph no doubt said 'Mega!' (or something similar) to this wonderful idea, and sent Alhazen on an expedition to make maps and plans. But Alhazen was just one of many scientists who have discovered that things are easier said than done.

MAD MAPS

Unfortunately for Alhazen, his survey showed the scheme was doomed. He feared the Caliph's wrath so much that he pretended to be mad – *for nearly 20 years*, until the Caliph died! Then Alhazen suddenly recovered and became a famous physicist, doing brilliant work on light and mirrors.

Beep!

Err...nothing to report, your Royal Bananaship

SCALING THE HEIGHTS

1860 British scientists measure Mount Everest in the Himalayas. They say it's 8,840 metres high, and is the world's tallest peak.

1880 The second highest peak is declared as K2 in northern Pakistan, at 8,611 metres.

1973 Chinese map-makers revise Mount Everest's height to 8,848 metres.

1987 In **March**, US satellites measure K2 as at least 8,858 metres – it's now taller than Everest! In **August**, the Chinese disagree, saying Everest is still 8,848 metres and K2 is 8,611 metres. In **October**, more satellite measurements make Everest even taller, at 8,863 metres. But K2 gets smaller, at 8,607 metres.

Let's leave the arguments there, and have a look at the theory of 'Continental Drift'.

DRIFTING APART

The theory of 'Continental Drift' was suggested by Alfred Wegener in 1912. He said that there was once a single super-continent on Earth. About 200 million years ago, it had split up and the Earth's land masses had gradually drifted apart. By the 1920s, experts were pooh-poohing these suggestions. Some insisted Wegener be banned from writing scientific articles or attending scientific meetings. Why such bad feeling?

✗ Wegener was a meteorologist, or weather expert. 'Proper' earth scientists were geologists. They did not like mere weathermen interfering with their science.

☝ Wegener was German, and Germany had been the main enemy in World War 1.

However, from the 1930s more and more evidence supported Wegener's theory, and by the 1970s the theory of Continental Drift had been accepted.

NORTH

SOUTH

...of course, it's all utter damned rot

AMERICA

EUROPE

17

Is There Life on Mars?

In the 1870s, Italian astronomer Giovanni Schiaparelli studied the planet Mars through his telescope. He thought that he saw lines across the surface. He called them *canali* in Italian, meaning channels or canyons. But the word became translated as 'canals' in English, with the idea that someone had made them.

Famous American astronomer Percival Lowell thought he saw them, too, and decided they were too straight to be natural. In 1895 Lowell wrote that intelligent creatures had dug the 'canals', to bring water from the planet's frozen poles to the desert-like central regions. More recently, some observers claim that a huge face-shaped area seen in photos is part of a Martian city, complete with avenues and a pyramid!

FLY-BYS AND ORBITS

In 1976, space probes *Viking 1* and *2* landed on Mars. Their photos failed to show any canals. The Martian landscape was just dead volcanoes, jumbled red rocks, deep valleys and incredible dust-storms. It seems the canals were an optical illusion. The results of experiments to detect life were also uncertain. As *Star Trek's* Mister Spock might have said, 'It may be life, Jim, but not as we know it.' However, scientists wanted more proof, so in 1992 they launched the multi-million dollar probe *Mars Observer...*

BEEN AND GONE – MISSING MISSIONS

In August 1993, the *Mars Observer* was about to enter orbit around Mars. Its task was to study the planet's surface and atmosphere in great detail. Suddenly its radio signals ceased. What had happened? Was it sabotage by Martians, defending their city?

The *Mars Observer* was not the first Mars spacecraft to go missing. The Soviet Union (now Russia) launched many unsuccessful missions to the planet:

Mars 1 took off in 1962 but its instruments failed during the journey. Two sister craft went off course in the same year and disappeared into space.

In 1964, *Zond 2* stopped sending signals on its journey to Mars.

In 1971, *Mars 2* and 3 went into orbit and dropped probes to the surface. These went silent on the descent, in the biggest dust-storm ever seen on Mars.

Four more missions went to Mars in 1973. One went off course. One failed to slow down and flew past into deep space. One failed on its descent to the surface. The last sent back a few vague pictures. Coincidence? Poor USSR technology? Or more Martian sabotage?

IS ANYONE THERE?

In the 1890s, Guglielmo Marconi invented radio. At once, listening for signals from outer space became the latest craze. Were aliens trying to contact us? In 1901, 100,000 francs were offered for the first person to speak with aliens. But Martians did not count. They were thought to be too likely!

We Are Not Alone

Many scientists agree – we are not alone. There's a good chance that life of some kind exists elsewhere in the Universe. Hundreds of people claim to have seen strange spacecraft and creatures from other planets, and millions of pounds have been spent studying UFO sightings. But, as yet, there's no proof.

Look – a reply from the gods!

FIRST VISITORS?

History is littered with legends of beings with awesome powers coming from the skies. In Peru, the Nazca desert is marked with patterns and lines several kilometres long. Were they messages made by ancient Nazca people to communicate with their gods or visiting aliens? Some people claim that the coffin of a Mayan king, Pacal, shows a spaceman who visited his city of Palenque, in Mexico, 1,300 years ago.

FIRST MODERN SIGHTING?

The modern age of UFOs – Unidentified Flying Objects – began in 1897 in Le Roy, Kansas, USA. A farmer claimed he saw a huge torpedo-shaped craft with a glass cabin below, occupied by six strange beings. It landed, lassoed one of his calves with a rope, and took to the skies, trailing the unlucky beast heavenwards!

FIRST MEETING?

In his 1953 book *Flying Saucers Have Landed*, American George Adamski said he had met a being from Venus, in the Californian desert. It was human-shaped with green eyes and long blond hair. Adamski said he later met other aliens and travelled with them to Venus, Mars, Jupiter and Saturn.

SAUCER PRINTS

For many years experts were puzzled by circles of flattened crops that appeared in fields. Did these corn circles show where 'flying saucers' had landed? When two men admitted they had created the circles, some experts refused to believe them!

First UFO fatality

In January 1948, staff at Goldman Airfield, Kentucky, USA, saw a bright disc-shaped object high above. So Captain Thomas Mantell flew his P-51 Mustang fighter to investigate. He flew too high, blacked out through lack of oxygen and crashed to his death. Did he get carried away pursuing a UFO – or did the object chase him?

SEEING IS BELIEVING

Many photos of UFOs are hoaxes. Some show car hub-caps being thrown like frisbees, or reflections in windows. And scientists have many explanations for UFO sightings:

✦ Secret planes being tested at night.

≈ Reflections in the sky caused by layers of hot air, like desert mirages.

⚊ Spacecraft and weather balloons reflecting the Sun, or meteors burning up in the atmosphere.

⚊ Earthquakes or powerful storms setting off bursts of brainwaves in some people. These brainwaves produce sensations such as floating, flying, leaving the body and being touched.

Not now! I'm looking for UFOs!

Space-The Final ~~Frontier~~ Straw

Space travel is one of the newest sciences. In October 1957, a Russian rocket blasted the world's first artificial satellite, *Sputnik 1*, into orbit. A month later, *Sputnik 2* carried the first space traveller, a dog named Laika, and on 12 April 1961 Russian cosmonaut Yuri Gagarin became the first spaceman. Since then, hundreds of people have flown into space, even to the Moon, and returned safely to Earth. But in this most exacting of sciences, there has also been the occasional dumb blunder.

Walkies! Floaties!

TILES FROM HEAVEN?

The NASA Space Shuttle blasts into space with the help of two booster rockets and a huge fuel tank for its own engines. After the mission, it glides back into the atmosphere and lands. Special tiles on its underside shield it against the enormous heat caused by the friction of re-entry into the atmosphere. That is, unless the tiles fall off. In early tests, the glue did not work properly, and the tiles had been slapped on carelessly by students on vacation work!

Err... Houston... I think we have a problem...

GET ME ANOTHER SPANNER!

In 1985, Shuttle astronauts repairing a faulty satellite discovered that its outer nuts were too big for their spanners. The satellite's makers had changed the design, without telling the space agency. It's not easy to nip out to the local shop and get another spanner when you're floating 200 km out in space!

PUTTING OUT THE RUBBISH

Russia's orbiting space station *Mir*, launched in 1986, has been visited by manned *Soyuz* spacecraft, automated *Progress* craft carrying supplies, and even the Space Shuttle. These spacecraft lock onto *Mir's* docking ports, and cosmonauts can crawl through a linking tunnel. But when a space-walking cosmonaut tried to link a special *Kvant* science module to *Mir*, he found that the docking port was blocked by a plastic sack full of rubbish from the factory!

HUBBLE TROUBLE

In 1990, the Space Shuttle launched the USA's orbiting Hubble space telescope. High above the atmosphere, it would give astronomers clear, sharp views of stars in deep space, much better than could be obtained from Earth.

But eager scientists found the pictures were blurred! Hubble's mirror was out of shape – it had been polished beautifully, but to the wrong curvature. Experts had noticed the error in tests, but it was so large, they thought the measuring devices were faulty. So NASA had to send another Shuttle mission to fix new lenses and correct Hubble's short sight.

C
ANY
OUREADT
HISEYETEST
WHICH WE ARE HOLDING UP

WELCOME

3

I don't think this is going to work, lads!

Impossible Fossibles

Fossils are the remains of animals and plants that have been dead for thousands of years. When people discovered more and more fossils in the 19th century, they realized that many types of plants and creatures had died out.

DROWNED IN THE FLOOD

The Bible said that God had made all life on Earth. So it was decided that fossils were the remains of living things that had been drowned in the Great Flood. The animals which still survived had been saved by Noah and his Ark. But then more fossils were found, even deeper in the ground. So the story was changed to two floods, then several, perhaps seven or more.

One of the first and greatest fossil experts, Baron Georges Cuvier of France, said that God had been dissatisfied with the living things on Earth. So He destroyed them with catastrophes such as earthquakes and floods, and then created a new batch of plants and animals. Lots of times.

It's so nice to be out of that smelly old Ark

CORKSCREW HOLES

Gold-diggers in the Wild West of the USA kept finding strange twisty holes in the soil, which they nicknamed 'Devil's corkscrews'. The burrows went more than two metres into the ground. Scientists were puzzled. They suggested the holes had been made by twisted tree roots, or even blasted by lightning. The real answer is almost as strange. They were the twisted burrows of a pig-sized beaver called *Paleocastor*, which lived 15 million years ago. Another prehistoric beaver, *Castoroides*, was as big as a pony!

BEAVER HOMES

HEADS OR TAILS?

Fossil-hunting is a tough business. You kneel on hard rocks in the dust and heat, bashing your fingers with the hammer as you chip the stone. At last – you find a fossil! So you take it home, and start to rebuild the original animal. After months of hard work you decide it was a beast with two heads, curly horns, three legs with hooves and two more with claws, and a tail on its chest. Why does everyone laugh?

The Rocky Mountains in Canada contain thousands of animals preserved as fossils, including one named *Anomalocaris*. Scientists once thought that its parts came from many different animals. Its circular mouth was believed to be a jellyfish, its long claw was said to be the body of a prawn, and its body was thought to be a sea-cucumber or a sponge. We now think that it was a 'killer shrimp' one metre long, with two great spiny feelers.

HALLUCIGENIA

Not all strange reconstructions are mistakes. The extraordinary worm-like *Hallucigenia* was named because the scientist who first studied it thought he was seeing things. It had seven pairs of spines and seven soft, bendy tubes along its body. We are not even sure which way up it was, or which was its front or back, but we know it was smaller than your thumb.

Dinowars

Dinosaurs were prehistoric reptiles. They first appeared about 230 million years ago, and all died out by 65 million years ago. It was not until the 1820s, when doctor Gideon Mantell and his wife found some fossil teeth and bones, that people began to study dinosaurs seriously.

MANTELL'S LIZARD

One expert declared that Mantell's finds came from an ancient rhinoceros. However, Mantell decided that they were from a plant-eating lizard, like an iguana but 35 metres long. His reconstruction, the first ever made of a dinosaur, showed it walked on all fours and had a spike on its nose. He called his find *Iguanodon*, 'iguana tooth'. We now know that *Iguanodon* was 10 metres long, probably walked on its back legs, and its nose-horn was really its thumb bone.

HEADS OR TAILS?

In the 1870s, many dinosaur fossils were found by American experts Edward Drinker Cope and Othniel Charles Marsh. Unfortunately, they were bitter rivals. In 1868 Cope had assembled the fossils of a swimming reptile called a plesiosaur. Marsh saw the reconstruction and pointed out that the head was in the wrong place – at the end of the tail!

THE BONE WARS

The rivalry between Cope and Marsh was so great they began a race to find dinosaur fossils in the American West – which wasn't big enough for both of them. In 1878, at Como Bluff, Wyoming, some men digging fossils for Marsh saw two strangers begin to dig lower down the slope. Thinking the strangers were Cope's men, they deliberately set off a rock slide and forced the strangers to flee!

The two teams found so many fossils – about 200 new species – that they couldn't carry them all. They smashed them up, rather than leave them for other expeditions to study.

HOW BRONTOSAURUS DIED TWICE

In 1877 Cope decided some fossils belonged to a huge new dinosaur which he named *Apatosaurus*. In 1879 Marsh found a different set of bones, and called them *Brontosaurus*, 'thunder lizard'. After many arguments, experts decided the two sets of bones belonged to the same type of dinosaur. So it is now called *Apatosaurus*, after the first bones named. Thus *Brontosaurus* has died out twice, in life about 140 million years ago, and in name by 1960.

A FINAL INDIGNITY

For many years *Apatosaurus* was rebuilt with the wrong head. Experts mistakenly used the skull of another dinosaur, called *Camarasaurus*, to reconstruct it. This head was tall, with leaf-shaped teeth. The real skull of *Apatosaurus* was identified in 1975. Its head was low, with peg-like teeth.

27

True or False?

The world of science is occasionally startled by a new and unexpected discovery. Then it is stunned, even shocked, to find that the discovery is a hoax or trick. When Dr Johann Beringer found and wrote a book about several new types of fossil in Germany in 1726, he was understandably excited. Perhaps he would become famous! However, the fossils were fakes, planted by rival scientists. How would *you* have reacted to the following discoveries?

... and here's one I made earlier

THE 'MISSING LINK'

In 1912, amateur fossil hunter Charles Dawson found bones and tools in the ancient gravels of Piltdown, Sussex. There were parts of a skull, and a lower jaw with teeth. British experts were overjoyed. Here was 'Piltdown Man', the 'missing link' in the evolution of humans from apes, from two million years ago. His domed skull, like that of a modern human, housed his big brain. His strong, ape-like jaws and teeth were left from his evolutionary past.

In 1953, chemical dating showed that Piltdown Man was a forgery. The skull bones were human, but only a few hundred years old. The lower jaw and teeth were from an orang-utan – filed down, coloured to look prehistoric, and put in the gravel with the bones. Who dunnit? No-one knows. But Piltdown Man had fitted the hopes of many scientists so well that they had not checked the evidence properly.

BEAKS AND FUR

In 1799, scientists were given the dried skin of a strange Australian animal. It had a furry body like a water vole, but a leathery beak and webbed feet like a duck! The experts were sure it was fake, since they had often been shown amazing creatures that turned out to be the sewn-together skins of different animals.

The experts tried to prise off the beak – but it would not budge! This was no fake. It was the first platypus examined by scientists. It was a mammal, with fur, and milk for its babies. But it had a bird-like beak and webbed feet, and laid bird-type eggs.

Frankly, I just can't see what's so funny

THE SEARCH FOR NESSIE

Tales have been told for centuries of a large creature living in Loch Ness, Scotland's deepest lake. The first recorded sighting was in 565 AD. Saint Columba said he'd attended the burial of a man apparently bitten by a huge monster while swimming in the loch.

In the 1930s, sightings of Nessie increased when a new road was built around the shores of Loch Ness. Some people said the monster resembled a plesiosaur, a 12-metre water reptile from the age of dinosaurs. Others said it was like a huge snake. Photos show dark shapes on the surface. In the 1970s, an underwater photo showed a bulky shape with a diamond-shaped 'flipper'. But Nessie has still not been found. Some photos have been exposed as fakes, others could be waves or floating logs. Recent expeditions using submarines and sonar (echo-sounding) have not located the monster. But tourists still flock to the loch and even hire helicopters in the hope of spotting it. Do *you* think Nessie exists?

Cane Toads and Killer Bees

In the natural world, there are no animal pests. Animals only become pests when humans take them to places where they don't usually live, or when humans change the natural conditions of a region. As these two examples show, it pays not to interfere with Mother Nature.

PLAGUE OF THE TERROR TOADS

In the 1930s, cane beetles were devastating the sugar cane crops of north-east Australia. So the farmers introduced 100 South American cane toads. These huge toads had helped to protect sugar cane in Puerto Rico by eating sugar cane pests. It was thought they would do the same job in Australia.

THE TERMINATORS

But, no. The toads liked the Australian bush more than the cane fields. They did not eat the cane beetles, which lived too high in the cane for the toads to reach – and toads, as most people know, cannot fly. However, they ate other native insects and small creatures, and bred and spread at an amazing rate. This deprived other animals, such as rare marsupial mice, of food. The toads ate the mice, too, and almost anything else they could swallow. As a result, gardens are now covered at night with a waddling carpet of toads. In the morning, the roads are littered with their squashed bodies, run over by cars and trucks.

TERMINATOR 2

The cane toad's own defences have caused even more trouble:

✹ It can squirt a poisonous fluid from glands just behind its eyes, up to one metre, into the eyes or mouth of a molester.

☠ Its skin oozes a poison that can kill a dog or cat that tries to chew it. Even a quick nip makes the dog or cat very sick.

🌢 If swallowed by a bird or snake, the toad hisses and sucks in air to inflate itself in the predator's throat, and suffocates it. Then the toad lets itself down and crawls away.

Should we bring in another animal to control the toads?
Perhaps not.

INVASION OF THE KILLER BEES

In 1956, some African honeybees (which are quite aggressive, unlike the European honeybee) escaped from a laboratory in Brazil. They bred with local wild American bees, who were also quick to anger. The result was the even more aggressive and warlike 'killer bees'. If anything annoys them – another bee, a larger animal or a person – they swarm around it in thousands and sting it to death. Huge swarms of these 'killer bees' have invaded most parts of South America. They are now stinging their way into southern North America, terrorizing animals and towns as they go.

Pesky Plants

Plant biology may seem a peaceful branch of science. Unlike toads and bees, plants do not invade places, wipe out the local wildlife and cost lots of money, do they? Wrong! Plants can be every bit as pesky as animals. A weed is defined as a plant growing where it is not wanted. And you could not get much worse weeds than these.

KUD U KOMPETE WITH KUDZU?

The Chinese vine called kudzu has been grown in Japan for centuries, for its edible roots and to make paper from its stems and leaves. In 1876 this creeper was shown at an exhibition in Philadelphia, USA. Americans were soon planting it as a decorative 'porch vine'. In the 1930s, farmers grew it as food for animals, and to stop river banks being washed away.

But kudzu can grow with incredible speed – 30 cm in a day! It has spread to the American south, where it has choked huge tracts of land with its rope-like stems and hand-shaped leaves as big as dinner plates. Buildings and machinery lay abandoned under a jungle of throttling growth. People still chop it to pieces, try to dig up its roots, spray it with chemicals, burn it with flame-throwers, and even hold kudzu-clearing barbecues using the vine as fuel for the fire. But the weed can't be stopped.

Get off!

PRETTY, AND PRETTY NASTY

The water hyacinth looks pretty, with lilac flowers and elegant leaves. But it's the world's worst water-weed. Helped by humans, it has spread from South America to choke thousands of rivers and lakes. In one summer, 25 small water hyacinths can breed two million. These can cover an area of three soccer pitches with a two-metre-thick tangle of leaves, roots and stems.

This weed strangles other water plants, suffocates fish and other creatures, clogs irrigation pumps and ditches, blocks pipes and turbines in electric dams, and tangles boat propellers and dredgers. Its damage costs billions of pounds every year. One of the few ways to control this waterweed is with the help of manatees, or sea cows. They love to munch the 'orrible 'yacinth.

I think I'm in Heaven

A prickly problem

The prickly pear, a type of cactus, was taken to Australia to grow as hedges. Local animals could not stomach its spines – and it spread and spread. By the 1880s, over 30 million hectares of eastern Australia were a thick carpet of cacti, useless for farming. It's still a pest in some areas.

33

A Hole in the Head

In the Stone Age, people tried not to complain of a headache. One treatment was to chip a hole in the skull, to let out evil spirits that were believed to cause the pain. The 'doctor' hit a stone chisel with a rock, to cut through the skin and bones and expose the brain. Ancient skulls show that some people survived, because the bone partly healed afterwards.

THE HEAD-DRILL

Making holes in the head was called trephining or trepanning. In the Dark Ages, the doctor used a metal drill. He turned it by pulling a bow to and fro, with its string wound round the drill. If the patients lived, they were awarded the largest fragments of skull bone, and hung them around their neck as a lucky charm!

Are you sure about this?

NOT VERY HUMOROUS

Hippocrates was the most famous doctor of ancient Greece. He believed that good health resulted from a balance of four substances, called humours, in the body. These were blood or *sanguis*, phlegm or *pituita*, yellow bile or *chole*, and black bile or *melanchole*. Too much of one humour changed your personality and even made you ill. For example, too much blood made you cheerful, or 'sanguine'. Too much black bile made you fed up, or 'melancholic'.

TODAY'S SPECIAL · PHLEGM · YELLOW BILE · BLACK BILE · BLOOD

HIPPOCRATES FOR ALL YOUR HUMOUR NEEDS

Cheerful, or sanguine

Sluggish, or phlegmatic

Quick-tempered, or cholic

Fed up, or melancholic

Now come on chaps, it won't hurt a bit...

IT'S ONLY A FLESH WOUND

Roman megastar doctor Claudius Galen wrote many books about the inside of the human body. Yet tradition prevented him from using a knife to cut open bodies. So how did he know? He just happened to be the official doctor for the gladiators fighting in the Colosseum of Rome. He saw plenty of innards in that job!

HELPUX!

LET THE BLOOD RUN FREE

In medieval times, people believed that many diseases were caused by impure blood, or by too much blood in the body. The obvious answer was to let some out! So the doctor cut open a blood vessel and let the red stuff spurt for a while. Or he stuck worm-like leeches on the skin. These feasted by sucking out the blood, because that's what leeches feed on.

hmm... MORE leeches I think

Did Ye Know?

In ancient India, doctors were supposed to look at the inside of the body, as part of their training. Yet the law did not let them use knives on dead bodies. So they left a dead body in water. After a week, it was so soggy that they could simply pull it to bits!

35

Taking Your Medicine

Now, what seems to be the trouble? Headache and upset tummy? We won't bother to take your pulse and temperature, or measure your blood pressure. Instead, we'll consult your star chart, taste your urine and check the weather outside. Then we'll forget it all, and prescribe a potion made from toad poison and viper venom. Yes, early medicine was weird and wacky!

Mmm, nearly ready

THERIAC IS GOOD FOR YOU

Physicians spent centuries working on the recipe for theriac. This was supposed to be a cure-all, or 'panacea' (named from the Greek goddess Panacea, who was the daughter of Asklepios, the god of medicine). Theriac was originally an antidote to snake bites, called mithridatium after a King Mithradates, who tested it on his slaves.

The ancient Romans expanded theriac to more than 50 ingredients, including opium from poppies, and viper meat. In the Middle Ages, physicians added even more ingredients. They said that theriac had to moulder and mature for years into a thick, smelly treacle before you took it. If you lived that long…

EYE OF NEWT, TONGUE OF TOAD

In the Dark Ages, just about anything went into the brew for making medicines, potions and ointments. If the illness was in a certain part of the body, doctors used a bit of nature that looked like the part. So liver ailments were treated by eating a plant called the liverwort. Diarrhoea was treated by drinking the rusty-looking water from stagnant ponds. If the patient was cured, fine. If he died, there was no one to complain!

TAKING THE URINE

From ancient times, doctors thought that a patient's urine was all they needed to make a diagnosis. The doctor studied the urine's colour, clarity, runniness, frothiness, smell and taste, and knew the problem at once! The glass urine flask even became the symbol of the medical profession. In fact, this procedure, called uroscopy, had no proper scientific basis. By the 18th century it was becoming less common. Today, doctors still take urine, but for a wide range of chemical tests in a laboratory.

No, don't tell me, I think I know the problem

There's no place like home!

BREEDING AND BITING

Before people understood that mosquito bites spread a disease called malaria, they thought it might be carried by small bugs who bit them at bedtime. So people put the legs of their beds in bowls of water, to drown the bugs as they tried to crawl into the bed with them.

But mosquitoes loved these small, stagnant 'ponds'. They buzzed in to breed in them, right beneath the victims they would bite next! People also believed that malaria was caused by an unseen staleness or miasma in the air. Hence the name mal-aria, 'bad air'.

Alchemistry

The ancient Greeks, such as Aristotle, believed that everything in the world was made of four elements – earth, air, fire and water – combined in different proportions. Could these elements be changed, or transmuted, one into another? So began centuries of alchemy, searching for prizes like the Philosopher's Stone and the Elixir of Eternal Youth.

She doesn't look a day over 2,000

THE ELIXIR OF ETERNAL YOUTH

The search for the Elixir of Eternal Youth began in China over 2,000 years ago. Drink it, and you would live for ever, and always look and feel young. The Lady of Tai kept her looks for 2,000 years. But this was because, as soon as she died in 186 BC, she was preserved in a coffin full of brown liquid containing mercuric sulphide and methane gas bubbles.

THE PHILOSOPHER'S STONE

The main aim of alchemy was to get rich quick. What? No, sorry, it was to carry out valuable scientific research, just in case it was possible to transmute cheap, common metals like iron into valuable ones such as gold. Alchemists also searched for the Philosopher's Stone, a legendary object that would make the process easier.

Air

Water

?

Fire

Earth

EXPENSIVE FAILURE

Many kings were persuaded to pay for the alchemists' expensive research. In 1317, Pope John XXII became so fed up with alchemists, and their claims and counter-claims, he ordered that alchemy be banned. The alchemists never succeeded in their main aims, such as finding the Philosopher's Stone. But by developing new equipment and experimenting with chemicals, they contributed greatly to the study of physics, chemistry, drugs and medicines.

STOP PRESS ~ Aristotle Builds Nuclear Reactor!

The basic idea of changing one substance into another has also come true – after a fashion. Modern physicists have found that unstable, radioactive substances change into stable, non-radioactive ones. For example, a form of uranium becomes thorium and then lead, and a type of cobalt turns into nickel. These types of change happen in nuclear reactors. The alchemists would have been pleased!

Tea up!

Mercury madness

Isaac Newton spent his later years doing experiments to find the Philosopher's Stone. Like many alchemists, he used the unusual substance mercury, or quicksilver, a liquid metal. It is very poisonous and sends people mad. This may account for the fact that Newton behaved very oddly in his old age.

Truly Shocking Science

Have you ever got an electric shock after walking across a carpet and touching a door handle, or getting out of a car? This is due to static electricity, which is usually caused by friction and builds up on your body. If you touch something metallic, or damp, or the ground, the electricity flows into it instantly. It makes your body fizz and jump! (Strong electric shocks and electricity from the mains supply can kill. *Never* play with electrical equipment. See what happened to Georg Richmann!)

MAKING SHOCKS

Before 1800, scientists did not have steadily flowing electricity – what we call electric current. They made static electricity with machines called electrostatic generators, by rubbing things together, such as glass and leather. The charge was stored in a device called a Leyden jar. If you touched it – *Whizbang!* You could be knocked to the floor by the shock.

MEASURING SHOCKS

During the 1700s there were few machines or instruments for measuring the strength of an electric charge. So some scientists used the human body as a gauge. They measured how far the electric shock went up their arm, or through their body, or along a row of people holding hands! In the 1730s, Stephen Gray, an early experimenter, measured how electricity flowed through the human body. Unsurprisingly, he had trouble getting volunteers.

Remember NEVER try this at home, folks!

SHOCKS CAN KILL

By the 1750s, scientists discovered that a lightning bolt is a gigantic burst and spark of electricity. In America in about 1752, Benjamin Franklin flew a kite in a thunderstorm. The electric charge came down the damp string and through a key tied to it, into a Leyden jar. Franklin was incredibly lucky. In Russia, Georg Richmann copied the experiment and was killed by a huge shock.

SHOCKS FOR KICKS

Machines that worked by static electricity became popular for entertainment. On stage, showmen made huge sparks to amaze their audiences, and shocked dozens of people together. In homes, the first electrical games machines made people jump and their hair stand on end. How they laughed!

MORE SHOCKS

Electric current arrived in 1800, when Italian Alessandro Volta invented the electrical cell, or battery. Volta argued with Luigi Galvani about the nature of electricity. In Galvani's experiments, dissected frogs' legs twitched when touched with a metal knife. Galvani said electricity was made inside the animals. Volta said electricity was made by combining chemicals, and animal muscles twitched when electricity flowed through them. In a sense, both were right.

41

Suffering for Science

When scientists invent new machines or processes, someone has to try them out. Usually, the scientists do the testing themselves. They become 'human guinea-pigs', and take the initial risks. But, sometimes, other people get to be the brave pioneers – whether they like it or not!

> You're always hungry

There's a hole in my stomach

In 1822, a Canadian adventurer named Alexis St Martin was accidentally shot in the stomach. His terrible wound was treated by US Army doctor William Beaumont. It healed – but with a hole from the outside right into the stomach! For the next seven years, St Martin allowed Beaumont to push tubes and pads through the hole into his stomach, so he could collect and study digestive juices and foods.

Beaumont published his results in a book called *Observations on the Gastric Juice and the Physiology of Digestion*, which helped medical research enormously. He lived to 68 years of age. St Martin, still with his stomach hole, reached 82!

Baling out

In 1849, a worried 10-year-old boy sat in a strange contraption with three sets of wings and a boat-like body. This was a glider, the invention of George Cayley, a pioneer of aircraft design. The craft was towed on a string, rose like a wobbly kite into the air, and came down with a bump. The boy declined to have another go.

Four years later, when he was 80, Cayley made a much larger glider. He instructed his coachman to pilot it. The glider, which had no controls, flew unsteadily before crash-landing. The shaken coachman quit on the spot, saying: 'I was hired to drive, not to fly.'

> Hooray!

I bet he gets all the credit

THE FIRST VACCINE

Smallpox is a terrible disease that has ravaged the world for centuries, killing millions of people. Cows get a similar but milder disease, called cowpox. It was believed that people who caught cowpox were then protected against the far more serious smallpox.

In 1796, English physician Edward Jenner decided to test this belief. He took some fluid from a cowpox sore on the hand of a dairy maid named Sarah Nelmes, and pricked it beneath the skin of a healthy boy, James Phipps. Six weeks later he deliberately gave James smallpox. If the boy had died, Jenner would have been called a criminal, not a hero. But James Phipps did not develop the disease, and Jenner became famous. This treatment was accepted as the scientific beginning of vaccination, or immunization, to protect against disease.

SAVED FROM RABIES

Rabies is a terrible disease, caused by a virus and spread by animal bites. In 1885, French medical scientist Louis Pasteur was researching a vaccine against it. One day a young boy called Joseph Meister was bitten 14 times by a mad dog with rabies. Pasteur was persuaded to try the vaccine for the first time. Joseph received 12 painful injections – and he lived. Soon thousands of people were being saved from horrible death.

When Joseph was older, he worked as a guard at the Pasteur Institute in Paris. During World War 2, he would not let enemy soldiers into the Institute – and he was killed for his loyalty.

...errr nice doggy?

Beyond the Call of Duty

The first person ever to steer a glider in flight was German engineer Otto Lilienthal, in 1891. In five years he made over 2,500 glider flights, before dying from injuries sustained in a crash in 1896. His gravestone is carved with his dying words: 'Sacrifices have to be made'. Here are some more dedicated scientists who suffered in their search for knowledge and progress.

A life in the Ballance

Italian professor Santorio Santorio, a colleague of Galileo, was obsessed by the human body's workings. To study its ins and outs, from about 1590 to 1620 he spent much of his time in a *Ballance*, a tiny room suspended from giant weighing scales. He ate, slept, exercised, washed, and read there. He weighed all the food and drink going into him, and weighed and studied all the products coming out, including breathed-out moisture, sweat, urine and faeces!

Can you stomach it?

In the mid-1700s, Italian scientist Lazzaro Spallanzani carried out many important experiments on digestion. In one set of tests, he swallowed sponges on strings, so he could pull them back out when they had absorbed his stomach juices. Then he added different foods to the sponges and kept them warm under his arm-pits, to see how digestion happened. He even went to church services with his samples!

CRITICAL CHEMISTRY

Versatile Frenchman Antoine Lavoisier founded the modern science of chemistry. He showed that air contains two main gases, nitrogen and oxygen, and he devised the symbols we use for chemicals, such as H_2O for water. He also improved French farming and town lighting, map-making, education, and the tax and banking systems.

In 1789 the French Revolution began. Among the leaders was Jean Paul Marat, who had been a doctor and scientist. In fact, Lavoisier had once criticized one of Marat's publications! And the revolutionaries did not like Lavoisier's involvement in taxes and banks. So Lavoisier was put on trial and guillotined next day.

I'll finish it later

CUT YOUR TAXES

LA CHIMIE par J.P. Marat

BUNSEN'S BURNING

German chemist Robert Bunsen carried out hundreds of experiments and invented dozens of laboratory gadgets, such as the spectroscope and filter pump. But he suffered greatly during his work.

In the 1840s, he decided to make some compounds containing arsenic, called cacodyls. Bad choice! They are poisonous, smell awful and catch fire easily. First, Bunsen lost an eye in an explosion. Then he got arsenic poisoning, which gave him muscle cramps, severe diarrhoea, and some paralysis. So he moved on to new work – taking gas samples from volcanoes and inside blast furnaces!

The Bunsen Burner

Oddly, the gas burner named after Bunsen was not his invention. It was probably developed by his assistant, Peter Desdega, from an even earlier design. Also, Bunsen cared little for his appearance. One lady said Bunsen was charming, and she would like to kiss him – but she would have to wash him first.

Flapping and Falling

To fly like a bird – that has been the dream of people through the ages. Even now we cannot flap through the air like birds, and so we have built many machines to help us fly, such as balloons, airships, gliders and powered aeroplanes. But it has been a long and difficult journey down the runway of flight, with many broken limbs and expensive failures.

WRONG FEATHERS

In the 11th century, a monk named Eilmer tried to glide from a tower, on wings made of bird feathers. He crashed and broke both of his legs. Eilmer blamed the wings, which were made partly of chicken feathers – and chickens are poor fliers!

Err, aukk, squawk

IN A SPIN

In the early 1500s, all-round genius Leonardo da Vinci sketched designs for human-powered flying machines. One of them was an early type of helicopter, with rotating screw-like wings. But it did not have a stabilizing rotor at the rear, like a modern helicopter. The wings would have spun one way – and the pilot would have spun almost as fast the other way!

Err, ooh

What a flapping cheat

In 1809, Joseph Degen claimed he was the first man to fly like the birds. He flapped wings attached to his arms, and flew through the air with the greatest of ease. But he cheated – he was hanging by a rope from a large balloon!

Is it a bird? is it a plane?

No, it's a big flop. In 1903, famous American scientist Professor Samuel Langley spent $70,000 on a four-winged aeroplane, the *Great Aerodrome*, which looked like a giant dragonfly. In October, it was catapulted along take-off rails on a houseboat in the Potomac River, Washington. But the craft flopped straight into the water. Instead of flying, pilot Charles Manley almost drowned.

Langley and Manley soon made a fresh attempt – another immediate splash-crash-landing. The newspapers gleefully poked fun at their very expensive failure. A few days later...

...Flight at last

On 17 December the first true aeroplane flew, and it cost about $40. The *Flyer No 1* was built by bicycling brothers Wilbur and Orville Wright, based in Dayton, Ohio, USA. The Wrights made four successful flights on the windswept coastal sands of Kitty Hawk, North Carolina. The brothers planned more flights, but strong winds tipped the *Flyer* and it bumped and bounced along the sands. The first successful plane was bent and broken, only minutes after its great triumph.

Err, well done, Orville!

47

Chocks Away!

Since the Wright Brothers made the first powered flight, there have been many strange ideas about aeroplane design. No matter how many sums they've done, and how many models they've tested, designers have never quite known what would happen until the first proper flight. Would *you* have gone for a trip in one of *these* weird winged wonders?

TOO MANY WINGS

If one wing moving through the air could provide force to lift a plane, then surely lots of wings would be far better? The Multiplane took this to extremes, with 20 thin wings, like a flying Venetian blind. And fly it did, in 1907, but only on three short hops. On the fourth attempt, piloted by its designer, Horatio Phillips, it came down with a bump and crumpled into a heap.

I have a dream...

TOO FAST

The Messerschmitt Me 163 was a World War 2 fighter with a difference. It blasted at great speed high into the air, using a rocket engine powered by caustic chemicals. However, take-off used up all its fuel and so the pilot then had to glide the plane back to the ground. The pilot was lucky if he or she got one high-speed swoop past an enemy plane. And worse, if the plane's fuel leaked from its tank, it would dissolve the pilot in seconds.

Tally-ho! Wunderbar!

TOO HEAVY

The enormous Hercules H4 flying boat was designed by American millionaire Howard Hughes. It was nicknamed the 'Spruce Goose' because its frame was made of spruce wood. It flew only once, in 1947. Even eight engines could not lift the vast body properly. Now in a museum, it holds the record for the longest wingspan of any plane, 97.5 metres. In contrast, the Wright *Flyer's* span was just 12 metres.

TOO SLOW

In 1954, the Convair company declared their F-102 Delta Dagger would be the first missile-carrying jet fighter to fly supersonic – faster than sound – in level flight. Tests on models in wind tunnels proved it! But when the first F-102 took to the sky, it could not break the sound barrier. Embarrassed designers found that the shape of the fuselage was not smooth enough. They admitted that models sometimes fly better than the real thing, and had to redesign it with a better shape.

TOO DANGEROUS

Lockheed's F-104 Starfighter was a super-streamlined jet fighter that first flew in 1954. Pilots saw the need for its downward-firing ejector seat when flying high, so they would be thrown clear of the Starfighter's very high tail. But what would happen if they had to eject during take-off or landing? Eventually a more powerful upward-firing seat was fitted. But in the 1960s, over 120 Starfighters crashed on routine flights, and many pilots were killed. Worried airmen called this plane the 'Flying Coffin'.

Pheew! That was a really close shave!

49

Mis-Construction

Large construction and engineering projects involve lots of experts – including planners, scientists, designers and engineers. They consider vital questions. Is the project in the right place? Will it work properly, and reliably? And can it survive storms, earth tremors and other events? Despite everyone's best efforts, things still go wrong.

THE TAY DISASTER

The Tay bridge near Dundee, Scotland, was the world's longest bridge. However, the designer had fatally underestimated the pressure of wind blowing against it. In a howling winter gale in 1879, the bridge's central section blew down as a train was crossing. The train and 75 passengers crashed into the dark water below.

GALLOPING GERTIE SHAKES HER STUFF

The Tacoma Narrows bridge over Puget Sound, Washington State, USA, opened in July 1940. This suspension bridge, with a main span of 853 metres, was beautifully slim and elegant. Unlike the Tay bridge, it was designed to flex slightly with the winds. Local people nicknamed it 'Galloping Gertie' since it swayed even in a light breeze.

On 7 November a medium wind sent the road deck rippling and twisting. The undulations got bigger. People driving across in their cars got out and ran. In a few minutes the road deck was bending as if made of rubber. Finally the bridge tore itself to pieces and crashed into the river. One cause of the collapse was the design of the road deck. It acted like an aeroplane wing as it twisted in the wind, creating up and then down forces.

I got rhythm

THAT SINKING FEELING

In the early 1990s, Japanese engineers built the new Kansai airport on an artificial island. But the island began to sink into the soft sea bed, and the runway is now just 5 metres above the water. Engineers believe that the island will eventually stabilize, but they have had to use 900 hydraulic jacks to support the airport terminal!

MORE BUILDING BLUNDERS

2580 BC Half way up, builders had to reduce the angle of Pharaoh Sneferu's new pyramid. Today, it is known as the Bent Pyramid.

1968 New trains at Long Island, New York, were found to be too big to pass safely through the tunnels.

1970 A calculation error meant one pre-made section of the Westgate bridge in Melbourne, Australia, was built too short. When engineers tried to plug the gap with concrete blocks, the bridge collapsed, killing 35 workers.

SHOCKINGLY STRONG

New York's Empire State building was the tallest in the world when it was completed in 1931. On a foggy day in 1945, a B-25 Mitchell bomber flew straight into the side of the giant skyscraper. One of the plane's engines smashed right through the building, and many people were killed and injured.

But this was also one case where the builders had got it right. The structure was so strong that the massive steel inner skeleton was almost undamaged. Today, engineers say that the Empire State could have a steel frame less than half the weight, and still be safe.

False Starts

Imagine life without the car. Modern road vehicles are central to daily life. We take for granted the efforts of engineers and designers as they improve our sophisticated cars – striving for better engines, aerodynamic shapes and more comfortable interiors. However, the story of the automobile has also had its fair share of surprises, shocks and false starts.

GETTING UP STEAM

The first self-powered vehicle – called an automobile – was Nicolas-Joseph Cugnot's 1769 'canon tractor', designed to pull gun carriages or carry four people. But this steam-engined three-wheeler went slower than walking pace, and stopped every minute to get up steam. During a demonstration to the French army in 1771, it careered out of control, crashed into a wall and turned turtle. The generals decided to stick with horses.

RIDING ON AIR

The first petrol-engined car with pneumatic, or air-filled, tyres was a Peugeot. In 1895 the Michelin brothers entered it in the Paris-Bordeaux-Paris race. But they gave up after 90 hours, having used their 22 spare inner tubes and mended at least 100 punctures. The race had been won 41 hours before, by a car with the usual solid rubber tyres.

WORLD SPEED SHOCKS

The vehicles which held the first six world land speed records were not powered by petrol engines, like modern cars, but by electric batteries. From 1898 to 1899 they increased the record from 63 km/hr to 105 km/hr. As well as the danger of speeds previously unthought of, the drivers faced another risk – several of them received electric shocks from their machines!

Err...

BACK FROM THE DRAWING BOARD

Today, hopefuls spend a fortune and many years on the best technology that money can buy. Yet in 1924, Ernest Eldridge took an ordinary Fiat car, souped it up a bit, and reached 235 km/hr – carrying the extra weight of a passenger, on tattered tyres, and on an ordinary tree-lined road near Paris! Then he was disqualified because his car didn't have a reverse gear, which broke the rules. So he added a reverse gear and took the record at 233 km/hr!

Left on the right

Why do Europeans drive on the right side of the road? Because Napoleon Bonaparte told them to, in 1807. His idea was to prevent accidents when two horse-drawn carriages thundered towards each other. Why the right? Perhaps because the British – his sworn enemies – had always used the left side. Vive la différence!

A Life on the Ocean ~ Glug

It's a marvellous life on the ocean wave. As you relax, far from school or work, the sun shines from a clear blue sky onto a calm blue sea, and the boat rocks gently. Dolphins leap and play, and the long-winged albatross soars above. Wonderful! Unless, that is, you're on one of these unusual or unfortunate vessels.

BENT AND TWISTED

The *Connector* of 1863 had a clever design. Its three sections were joined by two sets of huge hinges. The two cargo sections could be detached for loading and unloading (like railway wagons), while the rear-most, powered, part went off to do other jobs. The hinges also allowed this long ship to bend up and down in high waves. Tests on a smooth, calm river went well, but they showed the sections would be impossible in a rough sea. And the ship would twist in high waves and snap the hinges. The *Connector* was never used.

ROUND AND ROUND

In the 1870s, the Russian navy built two circular warships, the *Admiral Popov* and *Novgorod*. They were designed to swing around quickly so that their huge guns could point anywhere, and to stay steady so the aim was accurate. When the guns fired, their recoil reaction could not tip the ship to one side. This part of the design worked well. But the ships were slow, and even small waves splashed over them, flooding the decks and damaging their plating. And in a strong current, they spun round like tops!

I said forwards, man ~FORWARDS!

ROCKED AND ROLLED

When the wind blows and the waves swell, a ship rocks and lurches. The unpleasant result: seasickness. The *Bessemer*, built in 1875, was designed by steelmaker Henry Bessemer, who suffered greatly from seasickness. The *Bessemer* had a passenger portion that could tilt on guide rails inside the outer hull. As the hull rocked and rolled, a 'steersman' controlled hydraulic machinery to keep the passenger part level. It worked fine in small, predictable waves. But the steersman could not predict big, irregular waves, and the anti-roll machinery was simply too slow. Passengers felt even more seasick than usual.

The *Bessemer* also had two front ends, so it did not have to turn around in port. But it crashed into a wall at Calais harbour, and was wrecked.

You always did drive too fast!

THE UNSINKABLE *TITANIC*

In April 1912, the *Titanic* set sail on its first voyage from Southampton, England, to New York, USA. It was the world's largest and most luxurious passenger liner. It was also designed to be unsinkable: it had a very thick, stiff hull and watertight compartments inside. Even God couldn't sink her, said one of the ship's owners. But, near Newfoundland, the liner hit an iceberg, which ripped open several of its compartments – and the *Titanic* sank. Of the 2,200 crew and passengers, about 1,500 died. The sinking of *Titanic* was one of the worst sea disasters of all time.

The loss of life could have been avoided. *Titanic* was going too fast in an area known to contain icebergs. And, because the great liner was thought to be unsinkable, it did not carry enough lifeboats for everyone on board.

Inventions

Every year, hundreds of hopeful inventors and scientists unleash their brainchildren on the public. Very rarely, one of these inventions is cheap to make, easy to use, reliable, fills a real need – and so becomes a part of daily life. Here are some inventions that took a while to be perfected, and a couple of unusual ones that were devised by famous scientists.

ALL SCREWED UP

The basic screw shape was supposedly invented by Archimedes, an ancient Greek maths genius. Later, in the 16th century, someone actually made a screw for wood-working – a headless nail with a twist along its length. Unfortunately, no-one had invented the screwdriver. So you hammered it in, and there it stayed. A screw with a slotted head, and a screwdriver to twist it in, or take it out, were not invented until 100 years later.

Oh, very clever. Now get it out

CAN THE CAN BE CAN-OPENED?

It is said that the metal 'tin can' was invented in France in 1804 by Nicolas Appert, to store food for Napoleon's soldiers. Or by Englishmen Donkin and Hall in 1811. Whichever, the can was stronger than the glass preserving jars used previously.

Unfortunately, the lever-jawed can opener was not invented until 1855, by Robert Yeates. Between times, people had to use a hammer and chisel.

SHOUT LOUDER, EDDIE – I'M SEWING

American Thomas Edison's inventions changed daily life – the light bulb, phonograph (record player), electricity power station and distribution grid, as well as improved telegraph and a better telephone. But his sound-powered sewing machine of the 1880s was less successful. To make it work, you had to shout non-stop at the top of your voice, into a mouthpiece. It was much easier to use normal foot-pedals. Quieter, too!

SEW!

WHICH BRIGHT SPARK INVENTED THIS?

For centuries, people used heavy smoothing irons to uncrease and smarten their clothes. The iron was heated near a fire or in hot water. When electricity began to arrive in houses, from about 1890, all manner of new electrical gadgets appeared. The first electric iron was heated by an arc, an intense spark jumping continuously between two carbon rods inside the iron. It fizzed and cracked fiercely. It could also brighten up the day!

Perhaps, however, it was an improvement on an iron that was heated by burning gasoline...

Izzy's Pussy's push-up PORTAL

Very few scientists deserve the label 'genius'. One is Sir Isaac Newton, who laid the foundations of modern physics with his laws of gravity and motion. His *Principia* (1686) is one of the greatest science books ever written. 'Sir Izzy' also invented the cat flap!

Just an Accident

Scientists make mistakes and have accidents, like anyone else. Usually this means they have to start again. But occasionally an accident has led to a lucky break and a great new discovery.

PERKIN'S PURPLE PATCH

In 1856, a clever student chemist called William Perkin was working in his home laboratory. His experiment, to make the drug quinine from a substance called aniline, failed horribly. He was left with a disgusting black goo. So he tried boiling it – and it turned brilliant purple! Perkin realized this substance, later called mauve, could be used to colour, or dye, things. Perkin's mauve was the beginning of a huge new industry, making dyes from chemicals in the laboratory. By 36 he was able to retire, a rich man.

X FOR UNKNOWN

In 1895, German physicist Wilhelm Roentgen was experimenting with a discharge tube (a forerunner of the television set). Roentgen noticed that a piece of chemical-coated card near the tube glowed when it was switched on.

Tests showed that a new type of invisible ray was coming from the tube. It could travel through wood, thin metal and human flesh, but was stopped by lead or bones. The new rays could be detected by photographic paper, so Roentgen used them to take a photograph of the bones in his wife's hand. For a time they were called Roentgen's rays, but today we know them by the name that Roentgen gave them – X-rays, the 'X' for 'unknown'.

I thought it was quite a good likeness

A STRANGE ACTIVITY

In 1896, French scientist Antoine Becquerel noticed that some of his photographic paper had gone dark, even in its light-proof wrapping. Puzzled, Becquerel spotted that the paper had been stored near a chemical containing uranium. Tests showed the uranium was giving off mysterious rays. Perhaps they were the new rays discovered the previous year by Roentgen? But no – Becquerel had discovered yet another type of ray.

We now know the rays as 'radioactivity'. This name was invented by Becquerel's colleague Marie Curie, who later discovered the radioactive substances polonium and radium.

How very interesting!

KILLER MOULD KILLS KILLER GERMS

In 1928, Scottish scientist Alexander Fleming accidentally left the lid off a small round dish of germs he was studying. Then he noticed the germs on the dish were dying. Fleming found that some microscopic spores of a fungus, or mould, had floated into the dish – and were killing the bacteria! Fleming identified the mould as *Penicillium*, and he called the germ-killing chemical it made 'penicillin'.

Fleming's work was taken up by Australian medical scientist Howard Florey and German chemist Ernst Chain. They discovered how to make large amounts of penicillin. It was the first antibiotic, or bacteria-killing drug, and it was used during World War 2 to treat the infected wounds of soldiers. Since then, penicillin and other antibiotics have saved millions of lives.

Mad, Bad and Sad

Good science does not necessarily mean good sense. Some great scientists have been more than a little crazy. They thought clearly and sensibly about their work. But they were far less successful in other areas of life. Perhaps a dash of madness, badness or sadness is the price of a stroke of genius.

THE MAD MINERALOGIST

Rock-and-mineral expert William Buckland was one of the first people to reconstruct – rebuild – prehistoric animals from their fossilized remains. He wrote the very first description of a dinosaur, which he called *Megalosaurus*. In 1824 he suggested that it was a giant meat-eating lizard – an inspired guess, since the name 'dinosaur' was not invented until 1841.

But Buckland was strangely keen on coprolites, rock-hard droppings from prehistoric animals. He liked to shock friends by stroking the fossil faeces, and his dining table was made from huge rocks of dino-dung. He also wanted to try eating every creature in the whole animal kingdom! Buckland said the worst taste was mole meat, followed by bluebottles. He also tried mice in batter, crocodile, jackal and many other dishes.

The Stomach, Sir, rules the World!

excuse me...

...suddenly I don't feel hungry

... so take two *#~## swords twice a *#~## day!

THE BAD-LANGUAGE DOCTOR

Paracelsus was a famous 16th-century doctor in Basle, Switzerland. (His real name was Philipp Auroelus Theophrastus Bombastus von Hohenheim, but let's stick to the shorter one he liked to use.) He spoke out against the horrific treatments of the day, such as bleeding patients almost to death, and giving them dangerous drug mixtures of poisonous plants and animal venoms. He wanted to use medicines more scientifically. He tried them one at a time, in a logical fashion, to test if they worked. This was the first serious medical drug research.

But Paracelsus had his bad side. He said that the pain of a toothache could be moved into a tree, and that a sword wound was cured by rubbing ointment on the sword. He also believed in gnomes and nymphs. And he swore so much, and so offensively, that he was forced to leave Basle for ever.

ooh...err...

THE SADLY RECLUSIVE CHEMIST

Henry Cavendish made some very important discoveries in chemistry. He found that water was made of two substances, hydrogen and oxygen, and that air contains lots of gases. He invented ways of weighing gases. He also studied heat and electricity, and measured the force of gravity and the density of the Earth.

But Cavendish was eccentric and painfully shy. He avoided strangers, and could hardly stay in the same room as women. He was very rich, but he dressed in shabby clothes and ate stale food, alone in his room. He published little of his excellent work, and in 1810 sadly died alone.

Fame at Last?

The history of science is full of great discoveries and inventions. But the achievements of many brilliant scientists were not appreciated during their lifetime. Some never found fame – or fortune. Others got into big trouble because of their work. Today, with the benefit of hindsight, we can recognize their accomplishments.

Nice try!

THE THIRD BALLOONIST

On 21 November 1783, Frenchmen Pilâtre de Rozier and François Laurent became the first fliers, in the Montgolfier brothers' hot-air balloon. This was a blow to physicist Jacques Charles. Three months earlier he had tested a small balloon filled with lighter-than-air hydrogen gas. It had flown 25 km – but, on landing, villagers had torn it to pieces, thinking it was a monster! Eventually, on 1 December, Charles made and flew in a larger balloon. His name lives on, though, since he devised Charles' Law linking a gas' temperature, pressure and volume.

There... that's much better

TO UPSET A KING

Long before Jean (Luc) Picard, captain of the USS *Enterprise* in *Star Trek: The Next Generation*, another Jean Picard was travelling, around France. He wanted to calculate the Earth's size by measuring how much sections of land curved, using instruments he had invented himself. As we now know, his results were very accurate. Picard then drew the first detailed map of France, including all the coastlines. In 1682 he proudly showed it to his king, Louis XIV. Louis compared it to the previous version, and got quite angry. His kingdom was smaller than he believed!

It's mine!

TV, or not TV?

Scotsman John Logie Baird invented the television. True? Er, well... In the 1920s he invented a system for transmitting moving pictures. But his system, which used a fast-rotating scanner, did not work well enough. The all-electronic TV that we use today had its beginnings in the iconoscope, developed in 1924 by Russian-American scientist Vladimir Zworykin.

MORE PEAS, BROTHER?

Gregor Mendel was an Austrian monk who grew peas in his monastery garden. He bred different shapes and colours of pea plants by transferring the pollen from one flower to another. His painstaking work led to a great scientific discovery – the laws of genetics and inheritance, which he described in 1856. These laws apply to all plants and animals, including humans. They explain why features such as hair colour and eye colour run in families.

Mendel proudly showed his results to experts such as leading German botanist Carl Naegli. But they were unimpressed, and advised him to breed more pea plants. 'Pardon?' said Gregor, 'I have already studied 21,000!' Sadly he was sent away, and his research was ignored. Only in 1900, 16 years after his death, did biologists recognize the tremendous importance of his work.

Like many scientists before and since, poor Gregor had learned that the search for knowledge has its ups, downs, ins and outs – the world of *Shocking Science*.

Bill

Ben

You don't look much like your father

oh no, peas for lunch again

Index